CHILD CUSTODY: DOING WHAT IS BEST FOR YOUR KIDS

Find Out Your Rights and Learn Strategies To Communicate With An Uncooperative Ex

SAMANTHA EVANS

Contents

Introduction v
1. The Separation and the Children 1
2. Divorce: Good for the Kids 4
3. The Information on Rights 6
4. Dealing with Decisions 11
5. Consideration and Cooperation 16
6. Making the Most Out of the Situation 21

Afterword 23

Introduction

"Child Custody: Doing What Is Best For Your Kids" discusses you and your Ex's rights. It gives you strategies when communicating and working with an uncooperative ex. It is about doing what is best for your children.

Some of the topics include:

- Money issues
    - Medical care
    - Education
    - Religious training
    - Living arrangements
    - Holidays
    - Dealing with changes in an existing agreement
    - Working with professionals

1

The Separation and the Children

Having a marriage end may just be one of the most trying times in a person's life. Aside from dealing with the fact that the relationship has failed, one has to handle so much responsibilities that go with it such as the living arrangements, papers to fill out, division of properties and settlement of financial affairs. One may say that deciding who gets the house and what to state in the divorce papers are the most challenging parts to work on – but the truth is, nothing is as tough and complicated as having kids involved in this unfortunate situation.

Two people who are mature enough to accept that the marriage is not working out for them have an easier situation to deal with because they are the only ones concerned in the separation – if one aspect of the separation arrangement does not work for the other, they can always compromise or settle their differences with only their own interests to take note of. For example, in the dispute of who gets the house, one may say that he deserves to keep it because his family lives nearby, while the other may say that she should have it because it is nearer to her workplace. Whenever there are problems such as this, the divorced couple can always think of their interests selfishly without having any regard to other people or other factors.

But if there are children involved, their welfare and best interests should take preference over their parents' personal and superficial issues, no matter how important they may seem. In the given example, while both spouses have their own rational reasons in keeping the houses to themselves, in the end, the one who gets to stay with the children usually ends up keeping the house. The reason for this is simply for the convenience of the children; whatever will be more comfortable and better for them will always be the choice, even if it is not favorable to one of the spouses. Questions such as who gets the car and the division of the property will always take the back seat to the issues relating to the lives of the children. Yes, a separation is between the parents but it should not be forgotten that it is more stressful for their children.

Although it is true that it is toilsome for both parties to resolve the matters of their break up and that they should be given enough time and space to adjust each other's lives separately, this should not be and should never be at the expense of their children. When parents split up, children are equally affected too. They go through difficult phases also and though they are not the people directly concerned in such separation, feelings of guilt and hate will most likely develop within them.

Because they are still naïve and do not wholly understand the concept of separation or divorce, kids tend to think that they are at fault for whatever happened to their parents' marriages. Though there are some kids who easily gets used to the change of situation, there are still many of those who cannot. Several children go to the extremes of even hurting themselves as punishment for their parents' break up. Therefore, parents should cautiously watch out for signs of odd behavior among their children, especially at the onset of the separation. However, if it becomes difficult for separated parents to monitor their kids' behavior or make them understand, they can always avail of professional help.

Dealing with one's divorce is tough enough but that does not mean that one should disregard the effects that such divorce has on their children too. Responsible parents who deal with separations should always remember that the divorce only cuts their ties as husbands and wives but never their roles as fathers and mothers.

2

Divorce: Good for the Kids

People who go through divorce feel a sense of regret whenever they think of the welfare of their children. *Would things have worked had I stayed in the relationship? Am I a bad parent for wanting out of a marriage with children in it? Did I give up too fast? Do my children hate me?* These are just some of the few but usual questions that a parent might linger on whenever he thinks of the said divorce.

Although it is correct that some couples stay together for their kids, as it is better for the children to have both parents with them than to have a broken home, one should remember that it is not always the best option. Yes, the children will grow up in a home where both mommy and daddy are present but they will also grow up in a house where there are daily arguments, constant bickering, and innate hate for one another – and this is not favorable to for their well-being, especially if they are too young to understand what is going on between their parents.

Separation is an unpleasant thing to accept but in some perspectives, it may be a path to a better life. It is healthier for the children to see their parents live separately but agree mutually, than see them together in a house where all they ever do is fight, and it is a lot more harmful for a child's well-being to see and experience violence and hate in their home as compared to seeing their parents live in different houses.

In a study done between children of broken marriages and those whose parents stayed together despite mutual hate for each other, it was found that the former have better and more trusting relationships with their own partners than those who grew up with their parents living together. It has similarly been established that children who grew up with separated parents had trouble in the beginning, but they subsequently coped well with some of the harsh truth about relationships. Meanwhile, those whose parents stayed despite constant fights are said to get trust issues, they think that every relationship they have will be like the one their parents had.

Parents should forego the mentality that the children will be perpetually scarred by the separation, and despite the absence of love and care for one another, the parents should stay together. Though there are some advantages to staying together for the kids, it is not always effective for every situation. Yes, the children will be deeply affected by the divorce but soon enough, they will understand why their parents had to go through it, and why it was the better option for everyone involved.

Parents should always remember that it is not the separation that molds their children – it is the parents themselves. It is how they deal with the situation through their efforts that will make life easier and comfortable for their kids. At the present time, there will be problems and misunderstandings but with the right attitude and persevering ways, things will definitely improve.

3

The Information on Rights

Dealing with an ex-spouse is quite tricky and also challenging most of the time because of the strained relationship caused by the separation. Unfortunately, one is without a choice when the matter to deal with concerns the welfare of the children.

One of the problems that divorced couples deal with has a lot to do with exercising their rights over their children. Who has superior rights? What are the limitations? Should they share custody over the children or will it be better if only one of them have custodial rights? The quick fix that most divorced parents employ is to just compromise so their children can live harmoniously and peacefully with least effect of their divorce.

For those who are either new to this situation or are having trouble dealing with both the separation and the child custody battles, the basic information regarding custodial rights is in this chapter.

. . .

- WHO EXACTLY HAS the rights over the children?

As parents, both the mother and the father are entitled to have child custody rights over the children. If the courts find that both can provide for a comfortable and stress-free environment for their children, without unnecessary complications, then they can both be granted custodial rights. There are instances, however, when only one parent is awarded such rights due to various reasons such as poor parenting skills, lack of financial support, and abandonment. When this happens, the rights that the neglecting parent may either become limited or in the worst case scenario, they may be revoked, as suitably determined by courts.

Moreover, in situations where both parents are equally unable to satisfactorily perform their parental duties and obligations, child custody rights can be awarded to relatives such as the grandparents or aunts and uncles of the children, or the family court, will appoint a suitable guardian.

- WHAT ARE these child custody rights?

There are two basic child custody rights, namely: Physical child custody rights and Legal child custody rights. The former deals with the actual taking care of the children and the daily living arrangements whereas the latter is concerned with parental decisions as regards the children's important life events such as their education, choice of religion, medical care and others.

- HOW ARE these rights exercised by both parents?

Most of the time, both rights are awarded to the mother while the father gets to be participate in just the latter. The rationale behind this is that a mother is deemed to be able to care for the children better than the father, especially if the children are still at a young age. But of course, there is an exception to this case such as when the mother abandons her kids or if the family court finds that she is not physically or financially capable to care for them.

- DO the rights exclusively involve the children only?

Although primarily, the rights concern the children only, some of it nevertheless involves one parent. A parent who exercises physical child custody over the child or children has the right to demand support from the other parent. Hence, in some situations, it is not only the children who are being financially supported by the other parent but also the custodial parent who takes care of them.

The most extreme right that a custodial parent has is the right to change the children's names. This is not an ordinary situation and the general rule is that a parent cannot ask for the change in the children's names without the consent of the other, but there are allowances as provided for by the law. In cases where the non-custodial parent's rights are being removed or if the custodial parent just wishes to add her own name, the change can be asked from the family court, subject of course to a hearing and the evidences presented.

- WHAT ARE some of the rights of the parent having legal child custody only?

As for the parent who only has legal child custody, aside from being able to voice out his opinions and suggestions when it comes to parental decisions, he also has visitation rights. Most family courts award the other parent weekend visitations as to nurture the relationship between the children and said parent. It is very essential that the other parent be given this right so that the children will not feel alienated by said parent and at the same time, such parent can comply with his parental duties despite the separation.

These visitation rights may be modified accordingly to both parties' and their children's convenience. Although this right may sound simple, there are actually many disputes revolving around matters such as when a mother will not permit the father to see his children even in visitation days; or when a father constantly fails to show up on said scheduled dates; or when the parents failed to observe the court-ruled visitation schedule due to their personal issues.

- HOW ARE THESE RIGHTS DETERMINED?

These rights are usually determined by the court through the proofs of evidence submitted by both parties. Parents who have no trouble getting along usually pass their mutual agreement to the court and wait for approval. But for those who have to battle things out, the court has to go through tons of statements and proofs provided by both parties wherein they shall show how one parent is a better fit for custody or how one parent has poor parenting skills.

These are just some of the basic facts that one should understand about different child custody rights. Parents who are in said situation has to take note that acquiring the rights over the children is not a contest or a competition against one another and it is definitely not about who is the good parent and who is not – it is mainly about the children and what is best for them. Therefore, no matter what the issues are between the parents, it is very important that they work around it so that they could raise their children properly and agreeably.

4

Dealing with Decisions

Part of being a parent's many responsibilities is coming up with decisions that will be best for the children. This is easy when both parents mutually approve of each other's opinions and have no ill-feelings towards each other. But when the parents just came out of a bitter and unpleasant separation or divorce, this may be a challenge.

Having irreconcilable differences is one of the common answers that divorced couples provide when asked what caused their separation. Change of religious views, political opinions or even the choice of lifestyle are just some of the differences that couples find it hard to resolve so they end up getting divorced. But these should be kept back when there are children involved and their welfare is at stake. Having legal child custody rights over the children means exercising the privilege of making parental decisions and even if it seems hard to work with an ex, one will just have to do so for his children's benefit.

In this chapter, we will provide for four basic matters that concerns parental decisions and how divorced couples can work on it.

LIVING arrangements

It is a given that one parent would inevitably move out from the family home but the question of who stays with the kids is always a tricky matter. Most courts have decided that the children should stay with their mothers until they are old enough to decide to whom they want to live with; until then, the father shall settle with visiting dates. Nonetheless, it is important to point that although one parent will be staying with the children, it is crucial that the other parent live not too far away. The reason behind this is for regular visitation and to avoid straining the relationship between the children and the other parent. As much as possible, the living arrangement that the parents should agree on would cater to and focus on maintaining a healthy relationship among the family.

When a parent is living with the children, it does not necessarily mean that the other has no say with the living arrangements. The "non-custodial" parent has the right to concern himself with house matters involving his kids. For instance, if the non-custodial parent finds that the neighborhood that his children are living in is not safe, he can voice out his apprehensions as it involves the welfare of his children. Another instance would be if the "custodial parent", as what we shall call the parent who actually lives with the children, starts dating again and this relationship is potentially harmful to the children. In cases like this, the non-custodial parent can also express his concern without necessarily meddling with his ex's affairs.

Despite living separately from each other, both parents still have the correlative duty to care for their children and to see that the latter are in a safe and comfortable environment. Where the children will live, how their lifestyles will be and who they will be living with are just some of the many living arrangement matters that both parents should decide on, together. If there be any arguments relating to these things, it is advised that they are to include a professional to mediate.

EDUCATION and medical care

Having the obligation to provide for their children, both parents have the discretion in deciding which school is best. Some parents usually let their children stay where they used to study prior to the divorce to lessen the need of their children to adapt. But there are also those who transfer their children for various reasons, the two most common of which are: there is a great distance between the school and the new house; or there is a need to transfer so as to avoid the ridicule that the children will experience in school due to their parents' failed marriage. The latter situation is the usual reason why children transfer schools after their parents get divorced.

The same can easily be said about the medical care of children. Just like education, the children's medical care is a crucial topic that both parents need to discuss. What medical care plan they should get and what benefits are most appropriate for their children are just two of the things that parents should intently work on. In times of emergency, it will come in handy that the parents have already prepared a set-up so that there will be no unnecessary delay in providing for the kids' needs; how the bills should get paid, who is the child's emergency contact and of course, who gets to primarily care for the child in times of sickness or injuries are some of the things to consider as regards medical care.

Where the children should study, and how the parents

will provide for their medical care are two of the most significant matters that both parents should agree on because they are for the well-being of the children. Although seriously important, these matters are not usual sources of fights between divorced parents because both of them only want the best for their children so they compromise. Most parents deal with this situation maturely and every so often, they even let their children express their preferences.

But there are always situations when one parent does not agree with the other, as for instance when one's choice does not favor the other. When this occurs, both parents should remember that it is not their lives that they are dealing with but that of their children's – it is not their interests that are being discussed. It is not an issue of what is advantageous to one or to both of them; what is important is that the decision is best for their children.

FINANCIAL MATTERS

One delicate part of raising children from divorce is that the household funds are no longer conjugal; therefore, the kids tend to receive financial support from both the mother and the father. Some divorced families handle this aspect really well, with parents convening and agreeing that they should divide every expense into half so no parent will give less or more than the other. However, this is not what is happening in most divorced families. Most parents are competitive when it comes to money, as they believe they can "buy" their children's affections. Yes, the mutual obligations such as educational funds, medical bills are settled accordingly, but when it comes to giving allowances or gifts, then it can turn into a contest.

Whoever gives the child a better present or a bigger

amount of money earns the kid's fondness, especially when the children are still quite young and do not understand the concept of bribery. This is a prevalent situation whenever the non-custodial parent wishes to somehow connect with the child – he will be buying expensive gifts or splurging on grand vacations to make up for his absence. Although there is nothing wrong with spending money for the happiness of a child, parents should not make the situation a competition of who gets to be the better parent.

Also, parents should always remind their children that the things they receive from them are tokens of love, and there are no strings attached to them. If children are left without an explanation when it comes to these things, they tend to become spoiled. It is not the gifts that mend the relationship, it is the presence and active participation of the parent in his children's lives that actually counts.

When parents separate, they should keep in mind that though their finances are divided, they should nevertheless maintain that sense of impartiality when spending for their child. Whenever the topic of expenses come up, both parents should discuss the appropriate amount to be spent while taking into consideration the capacity of both to pay and the necessity of such expense. It is vital for divorced couples to acknowledge the fact that there is no rivalry, especially when it concerns finances. As in other things concerning their children, divorce couples should work together as a team.

5

Consideration and Cooperation

In the previous chapters, it has been established that even though divorced couples may work things out for the welfare of their children, it cannot be avoided that some problems or conflicts may still arise due to the differences of the ex-couple. Most exes fight over the smallest details such as who gets to pick the child up from school on particular days, or what the children should be eating and the most controversial of them all, who gets to spend the holidays with the kids. Child custody battles are very difficult and it cannot be avoided that some feelings will eventually get hurt.

To avoid the unnecessary quarrels and to help foster a peaceful environment for the children, here are some suggestions and tips that could help divorced parents work their quirks out.

- FIND A WAY TO COMMUNICATE WELL.

It is very crucial that the parents first work out their issues between each other so that they can properly work together in caring for their children. In reality, this is difficult to accomplish and may take a long time before it can be achieved so the next best thing to do is to ask the parents to set aside their personal issues whenever they are discussing their children's lives.

To start a harmonious conversation right after the separation, some divorced couples begin communicating with each other through non-personal means such as the phone or the internet, that way they can elude the awkward and painful meetings. In the earlier parts of the divorce, it is understandable that the parents will have trouble staying in one room and that these means, though conventional, will satisfy the need of the parents to converse, but after an appropriate amount of time has passed, it is advised that they meet personally so that they can discuss matters better, faster and clearer.

- HEAR YOUR CO-PARENT OUT.

When parents meet to talk about important matters regarding their children's welfare, it is very likely that some misunderstandings or arguments will develop along the way. This is actually normal and what is good about it is that it can somehow be avoided.

It is important for both parents to know that both their opinions are essential in the bringing up of their children so it is better that they take turns, hear out what the other has to say, and when they are both done, they can deliberate each other's views and suggestions. Both should remove the thought that the co-parent is doing one thing just to annoy the other. As said earlier, this is not about the divorce, but about the children

. . .

- ***ALWAYS BE REMINDED of the consequences.***

Some parents do not take things seriously because they are not aware of the consequences of the divorce. They just think that there will always be second chances and that their children are too young to even understand what is going on, this mindset should be avoided. Divorced parents must always remember that every decision they make affects their families, and especially their children. They have to be responsible and cautious because if they are not, the consequences are dreadful.

Parents should know that it is mandatory that they reach an agreement that works for them both; otherwise, not only do they put their children's lives at stake, but they also put their custodial rights at risk. Divorced couples who do not get along or even try to act civilized with each other are reprimanded by the courts. They do this by limiting their rights, or worse, by awarding the rights to other relatives or guardians.Consider the other person's feelings.

Just because the couple is separated does not mean that they can hurt each other's feelings now. It is a given that their relationship has already been tainted – there is no need to add further injury or damage to it. When talking about the children's affairs, both should be careful of their words and actions as to avoid unnecessary drama and problems. You should always put yourself in the shoes of your ex; consider your ex-spouse's feelings, even if it is difficult to do. It will definitely help the conversation if both spouses temporarily let go of the heartaches and trouble they caused each other and think of the good things they used to love about each other so it will be more bearable to work together. In the simplest terms, both should act mature and considerate, at least for their children's sake.

Also, considering feelings do not have to end with the

ex's – it is essential that the separated couple also consider their children's feelings. Do they feel caught in the middle? Do they have trouble coping with the set-up planned for them? Do they feel hurt? The children's feelings should be prioritized as the purpose of these all is to make them happy and secured.

- DO NOT CHANGE the situation rapidly.

People who go through divorce have trouble moving on because of their dependence on the failed relationship. Married couples who have been together for so long also take the longest time to recover from an unsuccessful union so whenever one has moved on earlier than the other, confrontations arise, accusations on being insensitive will be expressed and suspicions on infidelity will most likely be opened up. To avoid this situation, one should just give it time and let both the other spouse and the children adapt first to the divorce and its consequences. It is okay to move on, it is healthy for one's well-being but try not to shove it into the family right away. It is not easy to go from one circumstance to another so it is best to be extra sensitive and considerate and to just let things happen slowly.

- TRY to make things normal as possible.

If the pain is already bearable and both parents can now stay in one room without fighting, then family arrangements such as monthly dinners and vacation trips may be considered for the sake of the children. Children who come from broken homes crave for a sense of a normal family set-up and though this may not be granted to them absolutely, the parents could at least try, even for short periods of time to sacrifice their pride and provide a loving and non-hostile environment for their children. Take a vacation, trips or even have an in-house camping weekend – it does not matter what the activities are as long as the family gets together.

- *ASK a professional to help resolve the differences and the family issues.*

The worst-case scenario is that the parents completely disagree on everything; the choice of school, the people their children are exposed to and even the food provided for by the custodial parent. When this ensues, there will be a need to ask for help from other people.

There are a lot of family therapists who can help divorced families work out their problems so that they may somehow live in the best way that they could. By attending sessions, the family can ask for assistance on how to deal with the difficulties of a broken home, what are the effective ways for children to understand and accept the situation, and also, they can also ask for ways on how to move on as a family. Hiring experts to aid in this difficult phase also does a lot of help for the children as they are given the proper and professional attention they need.

6

Making the Most Out of the Situation

Dealing with a divorce is difficult for everyone involved – for both parents and children so it is encouraged that each should try to be sensitive and considerate of one another's feelings and opinions. When in situations such as this, it is better to feel positive of things. It is not the first time that families experience divorce and people who actually do so experience it turn out alright and well, so there is no reason to pessimistic. Divorce is already difficult as is so it is best to just make the most out of the situation.

For parents who wish to do away with cooperating with an ex when working on matters involving children, remember that is better to have a partner in tough and crucial things such as the children's lives and welfare. It is always better to have someone to talk to when a child faces troubles and failures so that this situation can easily be resolved and of course, it is also good to have someone to rejoice with when the children grow up well and successful. And also, one should be reminded that children need both of their parents and it would be unfair for the kids if either the mother or the father cannot perform his duties as a parent just because the divorced couple do not get along.

Parents should set aside each other's anger over one another and work as a team in making lives better and more comfortable for their children. The latter did not do anything wrong and was not part of the divorce, so there is no reason to punish them by not providing them with only the best in life. If things get too difficult and both parties find it hard to even be in the same room, then they should at least compromise.

As said earlier, divorce only severed the ties between a husband and a wife, but not the relationship among parents and children. The failure of a relationship does not have to cause the failure of another, specifically that of the parents and children because it is more sensitive and critical. After all, separated or not, a family is still a family.

Afterword

I hope this book was able to give you helpful strategies or ideas for giving doing what is best for you and your children.

Thank you and I wish you the best!